The BROKEN ANGEL

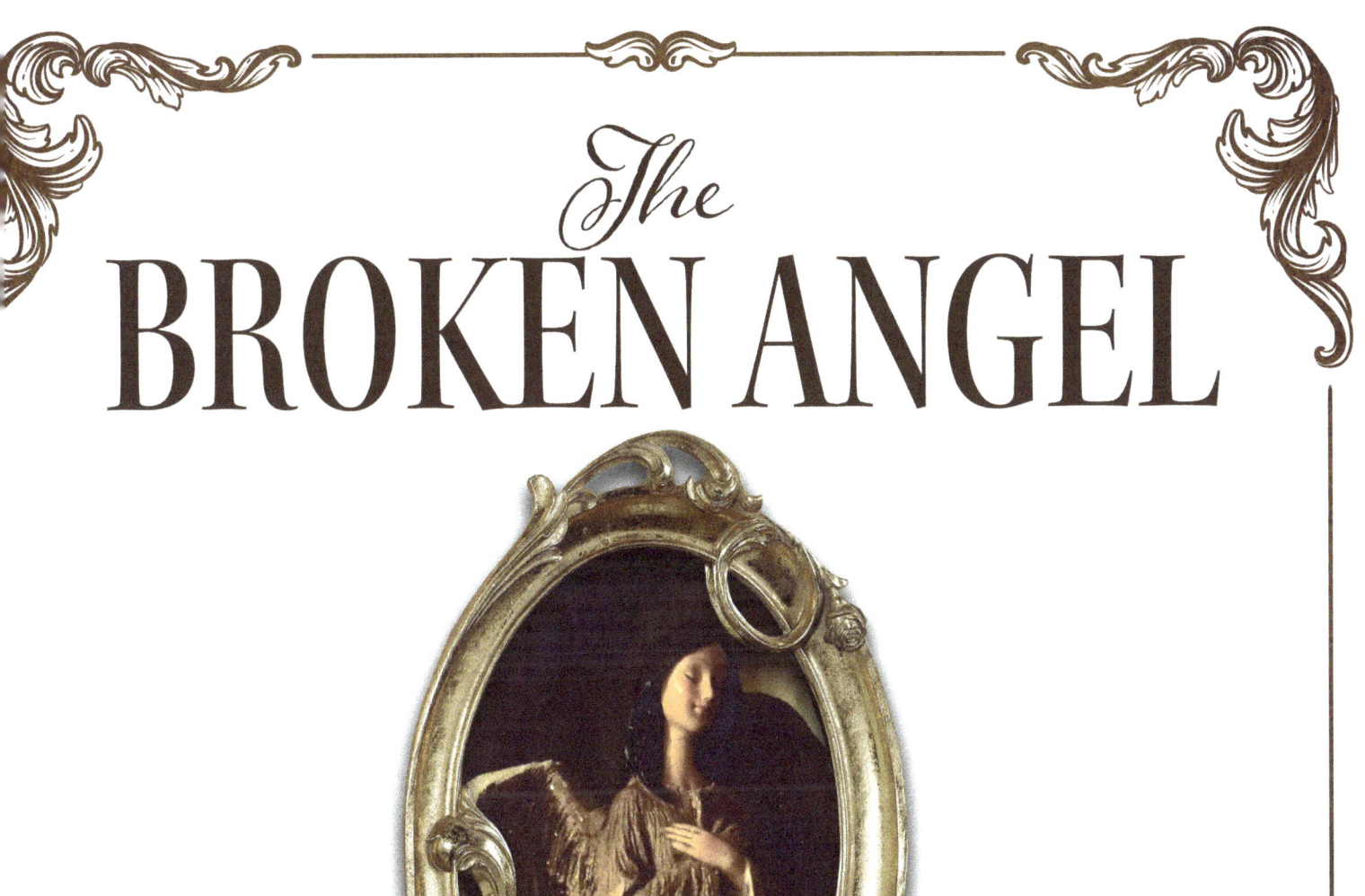

LYNN WATKINS

Published by:
Lynn Watkins
A Book's Mind
PO Box 272847
Fort Collins, CO 80527

Copyright © 2020
ISBN: 978-1-953284-26-6
Printed in the United States of America

No part of this publication may be reproduced, stored in a retrieval system, or transmitted in any form or by any means – electronic, mechanical, digital photocopy, recording, or any other – without the prior permission of the author.

All rights reserved solely by the author. The author guarantees all contents are original and do not infringe upon the legal rights of any other person or work. The views expressed in this book are not necessarily those of the publisher.

Website: www.redivivusministry.com
Facebook: https://www.facebook.com/LELWProclaimWord

The author wishes to thank those who made the illustrations in this book possible. These include the friends and family who served as photographic models posing and re-enacting events for the various illustrations. Principal photography provided by Captured Splendor Imagery. Additional material for the basis of some of the illustrations was provided by Goncharenya Tanya/shutterstock.com, KarepaStock/shutterstock.com, and El Design/shutterstock.com.

Ordering Information: Special discounts are available on quantity purchases by corporations, associations, and others. For details, contact the publisher at the address above.

Dedicated to everyone who loves Christmas and seeks its true wonder.

Christmas was almost here!
Our house glowed with Christmas lights.

The stockings were hung by the chimney.
The tree glistened, dancing in the lights.
A fire was laid
ready to burst all ablaze,
when all snuggled in for the night.

*I*N THE KITCHEN, THERE WERE DELIGHTFUL SMELLS;
FOR I HAD BEEN COOKING AND BAKING—
SANTAS AND SNOWMEN, CHOCOLATE AND SPRINKLES—SUCH COLORS!
MUCH TASTY FOOD FOR PARTAKING!

TURKEY WITH RELISH, APPLES AND YAMS—
ALL PROPER AND DUE FOR A CHRISTMAS FEAST
[TO RIVAL THE ONE AT THANKSGIVING]!

But for our dining table, I wanted something special –
Pine and flowers just would not do.
So, I went to the store, looking for something,
a little bit something more.

I did not know what I wanted;
I did not know where to look.

I wanted something special,
that spoke of "Christmas wonder".

That sparkle in the air,
when love and hope and "maybe's" make
all the Christmas lights
sparkle and dance
throughout the darkening winter nights.

The store was quite busy; shoppers, a bit in a tizzy.

*B*EAUTIFUL GIFTS GLOWED AND SHIMMERED WITH LIGHT.

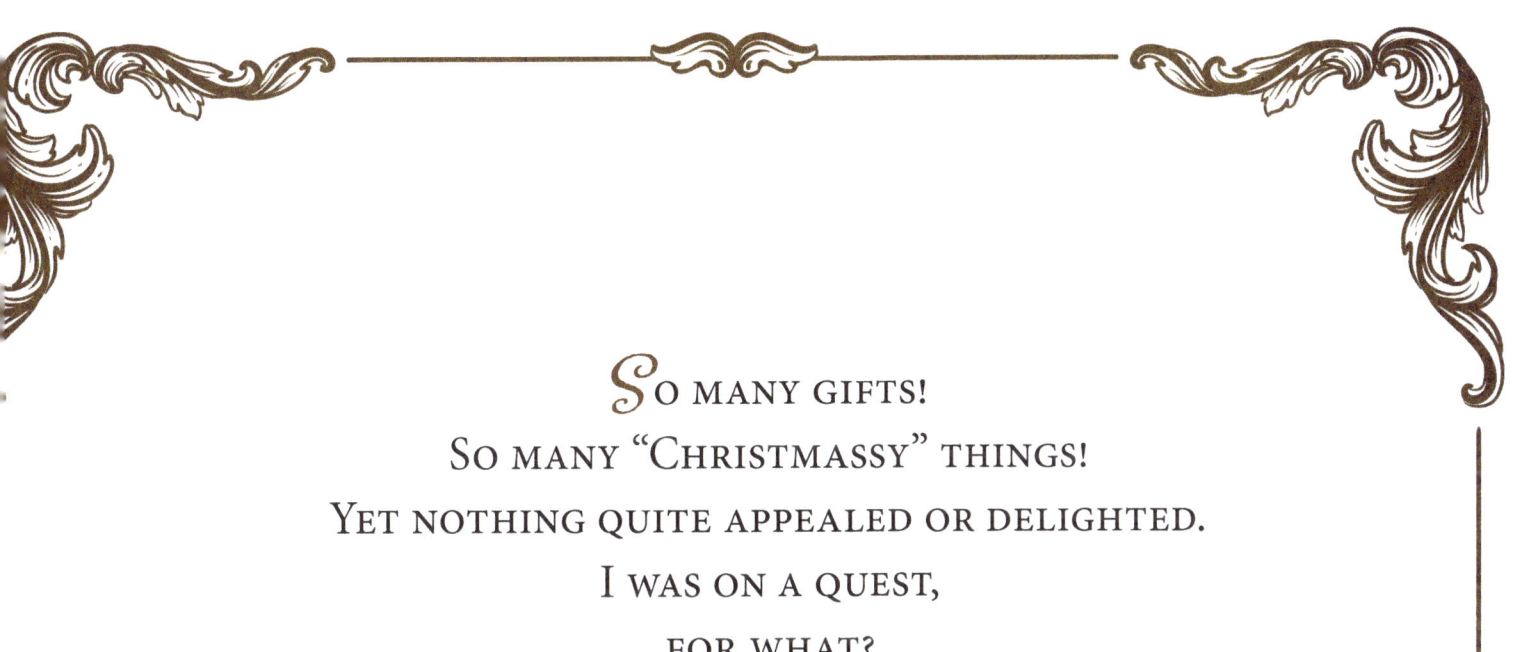

So many gifts!
So many "Christmassy" things!
Yet nothing quite appealed or delighted.
I was on a quest,
for what?
I could not guess.

So, I kept looking.
Until—
With my eyes, I did grasp
that beautiful,
graceful
angel
standing alone,
standing alone on the clearance shelf.

Her eyes! Her face!
She captured my attention.
I felt that I'd finished my quest.

Were there others like her?
Were many manufactured?

For me, it did not matter,
for there was nothing else like her
Though she sat on the clearance shelf.

She seemed so serene, so full of grace.
She seemed to be more than she was.
She seemed to be aware
of "magic" in the air,
And the wonder, the splendor, of Christmas.

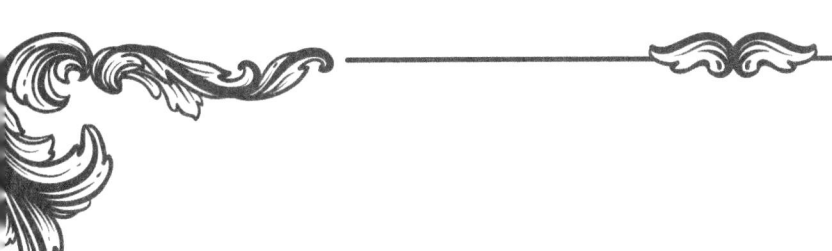

I picked her up
to gaze at her face.
A face full of serenity and peace.
I looked at that face,
her expression of grace....

[I must tell you,
I was smitten!]

I was going to buy her, when right at my side
a lady pointed, lamented, and sighed,
"That angel would be
so beautiful to me,
if ....

...HER WING WASN'T BROKEN."

I WAS HOLDING THE ANGEL IN MY HANDS,
LOOKING AT HER BEAUTIFUL FACE—
THAT FACE SO SERENE,
THAT FACE FULL OF PEACE.

However, I looked again at the angel. I turned her over. And, yes—her right wing was broken. It was as if she had lost her ability to fly. The sense of wonder and serenity I felt looking at the angel's face evaporated as I looked at her broken wing.

She was broken. She was no longer perfect. She'd been left neglected, to sit alone on the shelf; for in the eyes of all the busy Christmas shoppers—
including myself— she had lost her value. Broken, she was almost worthless.

And yet—I did like that face—
that face so full of peace and great grace.

So, I asked a clerk how cheaply they would sell me the angel. When he said, "I am sorry; there is no additional discount;" I left the store.

Yet as I walked to my car, my mind was a twirling thinking of the angel I'd left behind on the clearance shelf. I thought: How lovely she would be, if only she had been free of that broken wing! But [I told myself] Christmas should be special, for all our friends and family—beautiful to see, full of fun, laughter, and rejoicing. For this is the special day we all join in praise to celebrate Jesus' birthday. On such a day, only the best would do.

But then a voice spoke inside me;
That dear voice that I know so well.
That dear voice told me to stop,
To go back,
And to buy the neglected angel
Sitting on the clearance shelf.

"That broken angel means more
Than you thought,
means more than your
incorrect thinking.
That broken angel speaks
to all who will listen
of the Hope,
The Promise of Christmas."

"A Promise fulfilled—that God comes to find
the 'broken' to love and restore them.
The Hope that endures—He never stops searching;
He never stops loving,
all the hearts tossed casually aside.
The Lord sees beyond, so far beyond
the tiny, little flaws that you spy.

"He never stops saving;
He's always restoring;
till all that was broken is changed.

"Christmas reveals God's eternal, sworn promise;
His promise to come and to save!
Jesus came seeking to save all who were lost.
The broken restored—and He did even more!
The promise of heaven imparted."

Mathew 12:20 tells us that He will not crush the weakest reed or put out a flickering candle. Isaiah 61 tells us that Jesus is anointed and appointed to bring good news to the poor and to comfort the broken-hearted.

Jesus sees our value when we are broken and rejected as worthless by the world. Jesus loves us even when we reject ourselves.

So I went back to the store
to buy my "little bit more",
but now I could not find her!

I did not,
I could not, stop or give up.
For that which was worthless, was now, oh, so precious!

I searched, and the clerk searched
for that broken angel
on every shelf and cranny.
No place was too dark,
No shelf was too high. . . .
In a bin on the floor we did find her.

Ah, the lesson she taught me—
though she spoke not a word—
Of God's search for His own special prize.
So carefully, joyfully,
I carried her home
as a treasure no longer despised.

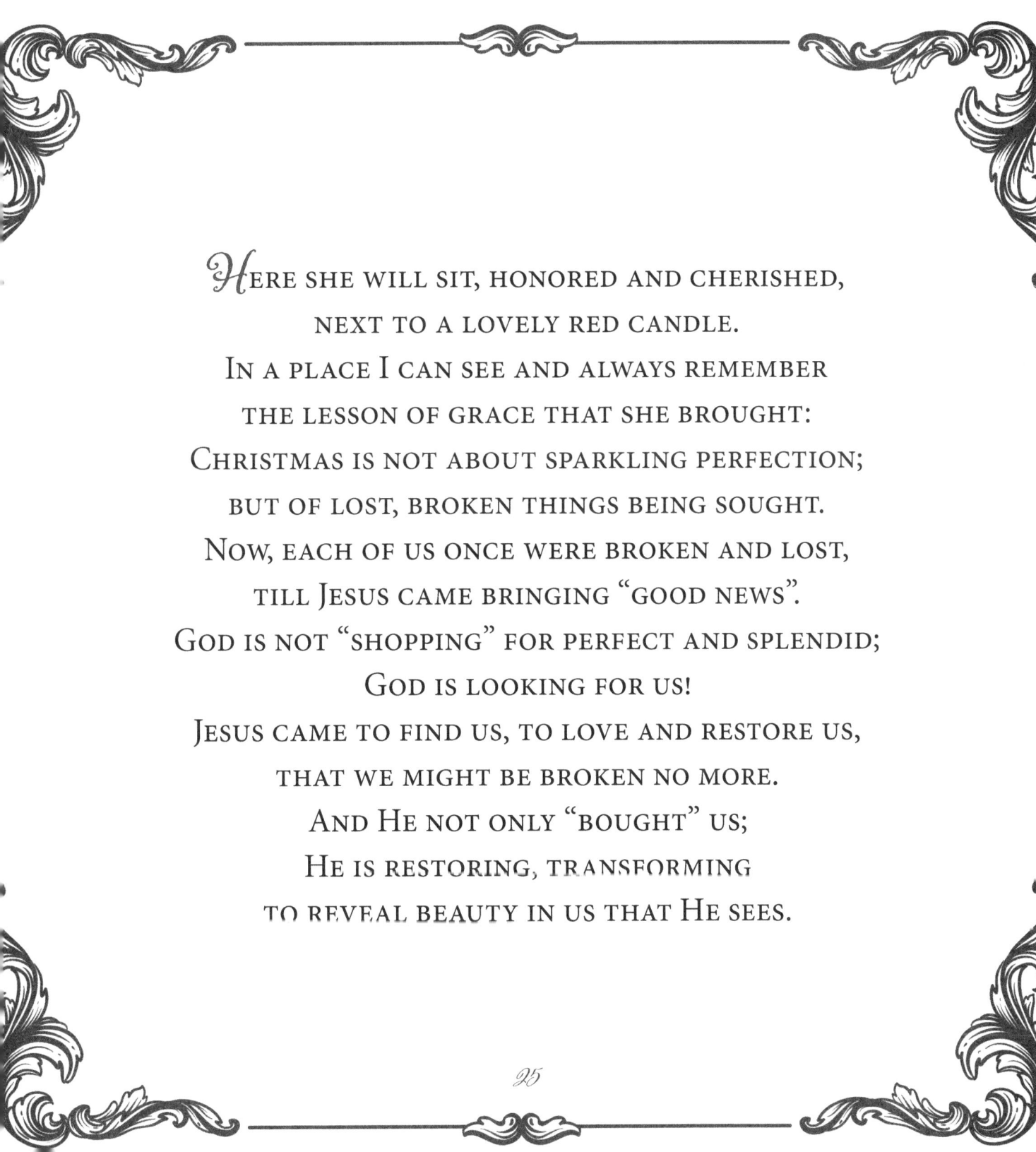

Here she will sit, honored and cherished,
next to a lovely red candle.
In a place I can see and always remember
the lesson of grace that she brought:
Christmas is not about sparkling perfection;
but of lost, broken things being sought.
Now, each of us once were broken and lost,
till Jesus came bringing "good news".
God is not "shopping" for perfect and splendid;
God is looking for us!
Jesus came to find us, to love and restore us,
that we might be broken no more.
And He not only "bought" us;
He is restoring, transforming
to reveal beauty in us that He sees.

And Christmas Day surrounded by lights,
With jingle bells lying so near,
We gathered round that broken, blessed, little angel
which now had become special and dear.
Her message of light and God's hope
in our night
gave spice to the feast on our table.

Have a merry, blessed Christmas!
But. . . .

Perhaps you thought God was angry with you. Perhaps you thought you had to be perfect to come to Him. Oh, friend, that is not true! Christmas demonstrates that God has come to help us and to find us where ever we are.
Jesus loves us!

Believe me: God wants fellowship with you. Please open your heart and let this be a merry Christmas like none you've had before. Discover the Light that shines in the dark; the Hope that never dies. Ask Jesus to come into your life and fill your life with His hope and joy this Christmas season. Jesus said, "Ask, and you will receive. Search, and you shall find. Knock and the door will be opened to you. Everyone who asks, will receive."
[Matthew 7:7-8].

How do you do this? Open your mouth and speak! Say, "Jesus, I have been told that You came to earth to reveal God's love and to give life to those who feel broken and alone. Please accept my brokenness and give me that gift of life. Today I choose to give up my way to trust You to do in and for me what I cannot do for myself. Amen"

*M*AY YOU EXPERIENCE GOD'S PEACE, HIS JOY, HIS NEWNESS OF LIFE TODAY!

CPSIA information can be obtained
at www.ICGtesting.com
Printed in the USA
BVHW021009181220
595406BV00007B/3